ANCIENT EGYPTIAN WONDERS

Mummification and Death Rituals of Ancient Egypt

William W. Lace

ReferencePoint Press®

San Diego, CA

© 2013 ReferencePoint Press, Inc.
Printed in the United States

For more information, contact:
ReferencePoint Press, Inc.
PO Box 27779
San Diego, CA 92198
www. ReferencePointPress.com

LIBRARY OF CONGRESS CATALOGING-IN-PUBLICATION DATA

Lace, William W.
  Mummification and death rituals of ancient Egypt / by William W. Lace.
    p. cm. -- (Ancient Egyptian wonders)
  Includes bibliographical references and index.
  ISBN 978-1-60152-254-2 (hardback) -- ISBN 1-60152-254-1 (hardback) 1. Mummies--Egypt--Juvenile literature. 2. Funeral rites and ceremonies--Egypt--History--Juvenile literature. 3. Egypt--Civilization--332-30 B.C.--Juvenile literature. I. Title.
  DT62.M7L28 2013
  932--dc23
                                                                    2012011481

CONTENTS

A TIMELINE OF ANCIENT EGYPT

Editor's note: Dates for major events and periods in ancient Egyptian history vary widely. Dates used here coincide with a timeline compiled by John Baines, professor of Egyptology at University of Oxford in England.

Great Pyramids of Giza are built by Khufu, Khafre, and Menkaure.

First pyramid, the Step Pyramid at Saqqara, is built by Djoser.

Capital city of Memphis is founded.

Upper and Lower Egypt unify as one kingdom.

Late Predynastic Period
(ca. 3100–2950 BC)

Early Dynastic Period
(ca. 2950–2575 BC)

Old Kingdom
(ca. 2575–2150 BC)

First Intermediate Period
(ca. 2125–1975 BC)

Middle Kingdom
(ca. 1975–1640 BC)

Hieroglyphic script is developed.

Old Kingdom collapses, resulting in a period of social upheaval and political chaos.

Egypt prospers during its classical period of art and literature.

Mentuhotep reunites Egypt.

4

Egypt enjoys peace for more than 50 years under Ramesses II, a noted warrior and prolific builder.

Ptolemy becomes king after Alexander's death in 323 BC; he founds a dynasty that rules Egypt for nearly three centuries.

The Rosetta stone, which later provides the key to deciphering Egyptian hieroglyphs, is carved.

Tutankhamun (King Tut) dies at a young age after a short reign; his undisturbed tomb is discovered in the Valley of the Kings in AD 1922.

Egypt regains its independence.

Hyksos rulers are driven from Egypt.

Persians conquer Egypt.

Hyksos kings invade and seize power in Egypt.

Nubians conquer Egypt.

Second Intermediate Period (ca. 1630–1520 BC)

New Kingdom (ca. 1539–1075 BC)

Third Intermediate Period (ca. 1075–715 BC)

Late Period (715–332 BC)

Greco-Roman Period (332 BC–AD 395)

Akhenaten introduces an unpopular monotheistic religion.

Alexander the Great conquers Egypt and makes it part of his vast empire.

Egypt is ruled by Hatshepsut, a woman pharaoh.

Cleopatra VII (better known as Cleopatra) serves as Egypt's last independent ruler.

Egypt becomes a province of the Roman Empire in 30 BC.

INTRODUCTION

Life, Death, Rebirth

L ife in ancient Egypt was characterized by constant renewal. All that was had been before and would be again. The sun—the great god Ra—rose in the east, set in the west, only to rise anew. The Nile River overflowed its banks each summer, bringing fertile topsoil for crops, and waned in the winter before rising again the next year.

This endless cycle of nature came to be reflected in religion. Those who were born would die and—if found worthy by the gods—live again in a lush underworld. A key to the afterlife, however, was preservation of the body, and this belief is nowhere better illustrated than in the ancient Egyptian legend of Isis and Osiris.

> **DID YOU KNOW?**
> Of the many versions of the Isis-Osiris myth, experts consider the one recorded by the Greek historian Herodotus in about 450 BC to be the most accurate.

Ra, king of the gods, believed that if his wife, Nut, goddess of the night, had children, one would end his reign on Earth. He placed a curse of infertility on her. But through the magic of Thoth, god of wisdom, she bore three sons—Osiris, Horus the Elder, and Set—and two daughters—Isis and Nephthys. Osiris and Set would later marry Isis and Nephthys, respectively, thus setting the pattern for royal brothers and sisters to intermarry.

Ra ruled both heaven and Earth, deriving his power from a secret name. Isis, however, wanted Osiris to rule, and she managed to learn the secret name. Ra's reign on Earth thus ended, and he ascended to the sun. Osiris became ruler and was hailed as a bringer of peace and plenty. The evil Set, however, was jealous of his younger brother and

The god Osiris, ruler of the underworld, is flanked by Isis (right)—his sister, wife, and divine symbol of motherhood—and Horus, their son, in this ancient gold statue. The myth of Isis and Osiris symbolizes the ancient Egyptian belief in the afterlife and the divinity of kings.

plotted to kill him. He gave a lavish banquet in Osiris's honor at which he announced that he had ordered a wondrous casket to be made from the most expensive woods and painted with gold. The person who fit best inside the casket would be given the extravagant gift.

THE DEATH OF OSIRIS

Set had secretly obtained Osiris's exact measurements. When Osiris lay inside the casket, Set and his accomplices slammed the lid shut, nailed it in place, and sealed it with molten lead. The conspirators then threw the casket into the Nile, and it was carried downriver into the Mediterranean Sea.

The grief-stricken Isis, determined to recover her husband's body, wandered the world in search of the casket. At last, in the city of Byblos in present-day Lebanon, she heard people talk of a marvelous tamarisk tree that had grown to immense size and which the king of the land had ordered cut down and used as the main pillar for his palace.

Isis knew at once that the casket had washed ashore, lodged in a bush, and then the spirit of Osiris's body had magically caused the tree to grow large. At length, Isis recovered the casket and returned to Egypt, hiding her treasure in a marsh.

Unfortunately, Set happened to be hunting nearby. He discovered the casket, ripped it open and, in a rage, tore Osiris's body into 14 parts and threw them in the Nile for the crocodiles to eat.

Isis once more set out to recover her husband's body. Aided by her sister, Nephthys, who had left her husband, Set, she finally was able to recover 13 of the 14 pieces. Despite Set's wishes, the crocodiles had not eaten them because of their reverence for Isis. Only one piece, the penis, was missing, having been eaten by a fish.

A SONG OF REBIRTH

Isis reassembled the existing parts and, through her magical powers, was able to fashion the missing penis out of gold. She then sang a song to Osiris that brought him back to life long enough for her to conceive a son, Horus. When Osiris was dead once more, Isis embalmed him, thus creating the first mummy, and hid him away in a place that only she knew. Reborn as a spirit, Osiris crossed to the underworld as ruler of the dead. His son, Horus, later defeated Set in a great battle and ruled on Earth.

To the ancient Egyptians, this story was much more than myth. They believed that their king, the pharaoh, was Horus personified—a god on Earth. When he died he became Osiris, and the next pharaoh took his place as Horus.

So it was that the bodies of pharaohs were carefully preserved and, with great ritual, sent on their journey to the underworld. In time the practice was extended beyond royalty, and everyone, even the lowliest slave, could hope for some form of immortality. Mummification, entombment, and the rituals that surrounded them became major parts of Egyptian life.

DID YOU KNOW?
During his battle with Set, Horus had one eye gouged out. He was magically healed by Thoth, god of wisdom, and the Eye of Horus remains a popular good luck charm in Egypt.

CHAPTER 1

The Evolution of Ritual

The notion of an afterlife—that death is but a transition to an eternal existence—is one of humankind's oldest and most basic beliefs. Nowhere has this belief been stronger than in ancient Egypt. As one funeral text proclaims, "You live again, you revive always, you have become young again, you are young again, and forever."[1]

To live again in the Egyptian version of paradise, however, required that the deceased maintain a connection between the land of the living and that of the dead. This connection was the physical body together with the various elements making up what might today be called the spirit or personality.

> **DID YOU KNOW?**
> A person's *ka* was usually depicted as a painting or a statue of the individual with a headdress showing two upraised arms.

Even the physical body, however, had distinct aspects. A living body was called a *khet*. When a person died, the body was known as a *khat*, or "corpse." It was transformed by mummification into a mummy, or *sah*—a word implying nobility or dignity, thus giving a person's physical remains an air of divinity.

The more spiritual side of an individual's makeup was even more complicated. It consisted of several aspects, some of which remain only slightly understood. These included the *ren*, or "name"; *shuyet*, or "shadow"; *ka*, or "alter ego"; *ba*, something like the soul; and *akh*, or "spirit."

THE NAME

A person's name was vitally important both in life and death. It provided not only something by which one was called but also served to establish the person as a living entity. To be nameless was to be no one—to cease to exist. To prevent this, Egyptians went to great lengths to preserve their names. Names were frequently painted or carved on the coffin, on the sarcophagus that held the coffin, or on the walls of the burial chamber. Friends and relatives who brought offerings of food often used bowls or pottery that bore the name of the deceased.

A person's name might well be a last resort. If the mummy rotted away or if statues of the deceased were destroyed, the name was

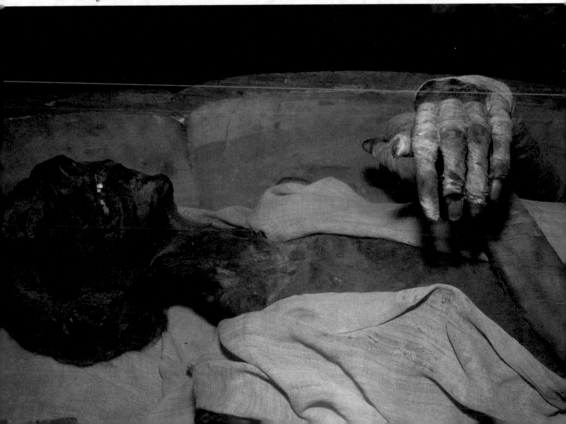

The mummy of New Kingdom pharaoh Ramesses II is displayed at the Cairo Museum. To fulfill the promise of death as a journey to eternal life, the ancient Egyptians mummified the bodies of their dead kings and entombed them in structures built and equipped for their comfort and daily needs.

thought to be enough to ensure eternal life. Even to speak the name was sufficient. According to an inscription from the tomb of Petosiris, high priest of Thoth, in the city of Hermopolis:

> I built this tomb in this necropolis,
> Beside the great souls who are there,
> In order that my father's name be pronounced,
> And that of my elder brother,
> A man is revived when his name is pronounced![2]

Egyptians also believed that the reverse was true— that if a name were forgotten or obliterated on Earth, the person would cease to exist in the afterlife. Some pharaohs had the names of their predecessors chiseled from tombs and monuments and their own names substituted. When the general Horemheb became king, for instance, he had his name carved over those of the two pharaohs who had preceded him, Ay and Tutankhamun. This was done partly for political reasons, especially if the new pharaoh and his predecessors had been enemies or if the pharaoh wanted to claim a predecessor's deeds as his own. But it could also be an act of vengeance if the objective was to deny the former ruler eternal life.

THE SHADOW

Like the name, one's shadow was considered an integral part of his or her being. Because the shadow seemed inseparable from the person, Egyptians believed it contained part of the person's makeup. The shadow's function in death is unclear, but it was thought to have the power to go forth from the tomb and roam the earth while the mummy could not.

The *ka* was even more closely connected to the physical body. The Egyptians believed that every person's *ka*, or *hemset* in the feminine form, was created at birth by the gods. The *ka* was a sort of spiritual twin that enabled a person to be alive. The word has been variously translated as a "life force," "soul," "spark," and "willpower."

"Gather the Bones"

The earliest forms of burial in ancient Egypt saw corpses placed in shallow pits dug in the desert sand, usually in a contracted or curled-up position. There, they would mummify naturally, dried out without decomposition by the almost total lack of humidity.

But near Naqada, a town just north of the city of Luxor and the Valley of the Kings, archaeologists working during the late 1800s discovered burials in which the bodies had no flesh and seemed to have been dismembered. In some cases, the skull was missing.

Some experts have theorized that these bodies were victims of tomb robbers or perhaps were dug up and pulled apart by wild animals, after which relatives reburied them. Sometimes the bones have been placed back in the tomb, but they have not been in the form of a skeleton. Instead, the bones have been sorted by type—ribs, fingers, arms, legs, etc. This custom possibly accounts for the phrase "gather the bones," which is found in texts many years after these burials.

In one tomb, however, some of the bones have had the ends broken off and show scratches consistent with bite marks. Flinders Petrie, the archaeologist who discovered the tomb in the 1800s, took this as evidence that the ancient Egyptians practiced some sort of ritual cannibalism.

The *ka* was thought to live on after the body died. It required sustenance that, after death, was provided by offerings of food and drink, either real or symbolic. Keeping the *ka* alive was vital for the deceased to be able to achieve immortality. Unlike the shadow, it could not leave the tomb.

Although the Egyptians gave the *ka* great importance, its exact nature and purpose remain vague. In death it took on several characteristics. A passage in the Book of the Dead, the primary Egyptian funerary text, reads:

> The Osiris X [the deceased], may he rest in peace, knows the names of your ka, the aspect of your soul that abides in the ground: Nourishing ka, ka of food, lordly ka, ka the ever-present helper, ka which is a pair of kas begetting more kas, healthy ka, sparkling ka, victorious ka, ka the strong, ka that strengthens the sun each day to rise from the world of the dead, ka of shining resurrection, powerful ka, effective ka.[3]

THE BA

Unlike the *ka*, the *ba* came into existence only after a person's death. Although it is sometimes compared with the concept of the soul in Christianity, many experts contend that the term *personality* would be more accurate. The *ba* included all the attributes that made the person an individual. Egyptologist Louis Zakbar went so far as to say the *ba* was not part of the person but was a spiritual manifestation of the entire person.

The *ba*, however, was not a purely spiritual entity. Egyptians believed that it had the same physical requirements and desires as the deceased. Like the *ka*, it needed food and water. It even possessed a sexual nature that it somehow was able to satisfy. The Book of the Dead speaks of the "Ba pure of body, health-embodying ba, ba bright and unharmed, ba of magic, ba who causes himself to appear, male ba, ba whose warm energy encourages copulating."[4]

Unlike the *ka*, however, the *ba* was not bound to the tomb. Like the shadow and sometimes accompanying the shadow, the *ba* could roam

> **DID YOU KNOW?**
> The Great Pyramid of Khufu at Giza weighs an estimated 6 million tons (5.4 million t). The individual stone blocks weigh between 2.5 and 15 tons (2.3 and 14t).

the earth, the heavens—sometimes accompanying the sun—and the underworld. It was usually pictured as a human-headed bird hovering above the coffin, ascending the tomb's shaft from the burial chamber, or perched in a tree above the tomb. Even though the *ba* could travel, it had to return periodically to the mummy if the deceased person were to live again.

THE AKH

A union of the *ba* and *ka* produced the *akh*, which was the ultimate manifestation of the deceased's being that took place at the end of the journey after death. A person could achieve the state only if he or she was judged by the gods to have lived an exceptional life. Those who achieved the important Egyptian concept of *ma'at*, or harmony and balance with nature and with other people, attained the status of an *akh*. On becoming an *akh*, a person became an immortal being associated with the stars. The *akh* was thought to dwell among the gods but was not itself divine.

The *akh* could, however, intervene in the affairs of the living, doing cither harm or good, and the word can be translated as "power" or "effectiveness." The *akh* could act directly on the living and could benefit those who set up some sort of chrine in the home or who brought prayers to the tomb in the form of letters to be left there. If something were beyond the powers of an *akh*, it might appeal to the proper gods for assistance.

Before the dead could help the living, however, it was up to the living to help the dead. People could achieve paradise—called the Field of Reeds by the Egyptians in most versions of the afterlife—only after negotiating a difficult and dangerous journey through the Duat, or underworld, to a place where they would be judged by the gods.

First Anubis, the jackal-headed god associated with death and mummification, and then Isis would escort the deceased to the Western Gate, which formed the entrance to the Duat. The deceased would then have to cross a river guarded by a monster serpent before having to pass through trials involving gates guarded by demons before reaching the place where Osiris would pronounce judgment.

HELP FOR THE DEAD

This journey through the Duat was impossible without the aid of the living. Not only were the deceased helped along the way by the prayers of friends and relatives, but they also had material aid. Even in their spirit form, the deceased needed food and drink to sustain strength. These could be left in the burial chamber or brought to an aboveground chapel. In addition, the journey might require paddles or oars for the journey across the river or weapons with which to fight off monsters or demons.

The most valuable tools, however, were collections of spells the deceased needed to ward off evil and pass safely through the gates. The earliest of these, dating from about 2400 BC, were reserved for royalty. Known as the Pyramid Texts, they were carved on sarcophagi and on the interior walls of the pyramids at the huge cemetery at Saqqara, located just south of the Nile River delta.

About 200 years after the Pyramid Texts appeared, lavishly illustrated spells known as Coffin Texts, also intended to guide the deceased through the Duat, began to be placed on the inside of wooden coffins. These spells were not reserved for pharaohs; they could be used by anyone who could afford them. And, because they were used in the coffins of commoners, some showed scenes of everyday life.

THE BOOK OF THE DEAD

By far the most widespread collections of spells, however, were those known collectively as the Book of the Dead. The Egyptians referred to it as the Book of the Coming Forth by Day, and the first versions date from about 1700 BC. There was no official version of the Book of the Dead. Indeed, there were thousands of versions because they were often commissioned to be written during a person's lifetime and were thus individualized to fit that person's circumstances.

The text followed the same general format as those that had been carved on the exterior of the sarcophagus, but the number of spells had increased to the point that they needed to be written and illustrated on papyrus scrolls and placed inside the coffin. Sometimes, to make sure the spirit had the proper spells close at hand, the scrolls were wrapped inside the mummy.

The spirits of the dead could not successfully complete their journeys without the objects placed in the tomb or the spells carved or painted on the tomb walls. For this reason Egyptians often spent as much time, effort, and money on their resting place as they did on their earthly homes. One Egyptian noble living in about 2500 BC left this advice: "When you prosper, found [establish] your household. . . . When you make a place for yourself, make good your dwelling in the graveyard. Make worthy your dwelling in the west."[5]

The human-headed bird that represents the ba *of the deceased appears in an ancient Egyptian tomb painting. The* ba *roamed the earth, the heavens, and the underworld but always returned to the mummy so that it could live again.*

THE POWERS OF THE DEAD

The ancient Egyptians believed that those who died not only entered another world—the afterlife—but also remained part of this one. Various aspects of a person's spirit were thought to revisit the place of his or her earthly existence and even influence its events.

The highest state a person's spirit could achieve was to become an *akh*, or "shining one," a star in the belly of Nut, goddess of the night, who was thought to hang over the earth. The *akhu* (the plural of *akh)* were generally beneficial to the living, but they could cause mischief if their tombs were ignored or if they were dissatisfied with offerings.

The Book of the Dead gives this warning: "Satisfy the *akh*; do what he wishes, keep yourself clear of what he abominates, that you may remain unscathed by his many hurts. Beware of every sort of damage. The cow in the field was stolen? It is he who does the like. As for any loss from the threshing floor, 'It is an *akh!*' they say."

Quoted in John H. Taylor, ed., *Journey Through the Afterlife*. Cambridge, MA: Harvard University Press, p. 23.

The west, where the sun god Ra departed from view each night, was associated with death. If land were available, Egyptians preferred to be buried in the desert west of the Nile. The desert was known as the "red lands," whereas the fertile soil on either side of the Nile was described as the "black lands." This narrow strip of fertile land was so important for farming that it could not be spared for cemeteries and tombs. In addition, these lands flooded each year, and dry land was needed for underground burial.

THE EARLIEST GRAVES

It may well have been the desert that gave the Egyptians the idea for preservation of the body and led to their belief in the afterlife. The earliest graves, thousands of years before the first pharaohs ruled, were shallow pits dug into the sand. The body usually was placed on its side in a curled-up, fetal position. It faced east, so as to greet the rising sun.

Bodies buried in the hot and extremely arid desert tended not to decay but to dry out. The muscles and internal organs might be reduced to almost nothing, but the skeleton remained, as did the skin and often even the hair. If these mummified remains were exposed to view by the wind or perhaps by wild animals, they might have given the Egyptians the idea that the body could be preserved and act as a link between the earthly world and what lay beyond.

These very ancient Egyptians are thought to have believed in some sort of afterlife. Pottery, beads, and tools were often placed in the grave, evidently for the deceased to use. In some cases, where only bones were left, they were very carefully separated and arranged by type. Some bore marks suggesting ritual cannibalism.

> **DID YOU KNOW?**
> The Book of the Dead is not a single work but rather a collection of funerary texts from various times and locations. The title was bestowed by archaeologist Richard Lepsius in 1843.

THE TOMB

The earthly home of the body—the tomb—consisted essentially of two parts: a subterranean burial chamber and an aboveground chapel or other structure at which friends and relatives could visit the deceased, bringing prayers and offerings. This arrangement was a mirror image of the Egyptian view of the world, with the burial chamber representing the Duat and the chapel synonymous with the land of the living.

Shortly after about 3000 BC, burial pits grew more elaborate. The burial chambers of pharaohs of the First Dynasty, or first ruling family, were lined in brick and contained rooms framed with wood. There were two aboveground structures: a simple mound above the burial chamber and an enclosed area nearby for ceremonies to honor the dead king.

At Saqqara some elaborate but nonroyal tombs combined the two surface structures into a single building with exterior wood paneling. Bodies were laid on their sides in a fetal position, but some were wrapped in cloth strips in an early form of mummification.

About 200 years later the paneling was abandoned in favor of solid, squat, table-like structures that resembled benches. Egyptologists call these structures mastabas, after the Arabic word for "bench." The mastaba was normally rectangular, with the long sides oriented north-south. There might be a small chapel—always facing east—with a false door before which visitors placed offerings. In later versions functional doors opened into a highly decorated chapel. Mastabas remained a primary tomb design for wealthy private citizens until about 1500 BC.

THE PYRAMIDS

Pharaohs' tombs, however, underwent a dramatic transformation. The burial complex of Khasekhemwy, the last king of the Second Dynasty, featured a mound-like structure with a brick exterior—the first step toward what would be the best-known example of all Egyptian tombs, the pyramids.

The transformation was swift. Less than a century after Khasekhemwy's death, the first pyramid, that of King Djoser, was built at Saqqara. From a central mastaba, the building extended sideways in all directions and then upward, finally consisting of six stair-step levels. Egyptologists Salima Ikram and Aidan Dodson call this pyramid "the first substantial stone structure erected by man."[6] It had a base that was 358 by 410 feet (109 by 125m) and reached a height of 203 feet (62m), with the entire structure covered in gleaming white limestone.

As large as the Step Pyramid was, it was dwarfed by those that came soon after: the three Great Pyramids at Giza. The largest was that of King Khufu; it was built over a 20-year period, ending in about 2524

About a century after the Hyksos people conquered northern Egypt, tomb building shifted from large aboveground structures to burial chambers carved into rocky cliffs. The most famous of these have been found in the Valley of the Kings (pictured).

BC. The base covered about 570,000 square feet (52,955 sq. m), and the peak stood 480 feet (146m) above the desert floor. It would remain the tallest manmade structure in the world for another 3,800 years.

The other two pyramids in the Giza complex (built for Khafre and Menkaure), although smaller, remain much larger than anything that was to come afterward. The pyramid of Khafre, Khufu's grandson, stood 448 feet (137m) high, and the tomb of Menkaure, Khafre's son, was much smaller, with a height of 218 feet (65.5m).

Changes over Time

The structure of the pyramids had religious overtones. Khasekhemwy's stair steps might have represented a pathway by which the king could climb to join Ra. Likewise, the smooth pyramids at Giza have been likened to the sun's rays descending to the earth.

Pyramids were not reserved exclusively for kings. Many queens had their own, much smaller pyramids, as did some high court officials. Egyptologist Richard Lepsius counted 67 pyramids in 1842, but desert sands had covered the ruins of many more. The last one to be discovered, in 2008, brought the total to 118.

Pyramid building dwindled sharply in about 1650 BC, when a people known as the Hyksos conquered northern Egypt. When they were expelled about a century later, it was by a family centered in Thebes to the south. This shift in the seat of power caused a change in tomb design. Large surface structures gave way to tombs cut into rock cliffs, the most famous of which were discovered in the Valley of the Kings a few miles west of Thebes.

The change came about partially because the terrain was not suited to large, pyramidal structures and also because of an increasing need for security. Royal tombs were magnets for robbers, and nothing—not fear of guards or gods—seemed to stop them. Akheperre, who died in about 1001 BC, is thought to have had the only king's tomb found completely intact.

Another change occurred in about 1330 BC, when surface structures reappeared near Saqqara. Instead of the mastaba design, however, the chapel took on the form of a temple, with a courtyard surrounded by pillars leading to a chapel containing a statue of the deceased.

The Tanis Tombs

About 200 years later, during a period of political instability known as the Third Intermediate Period, the capital of Egypt moved north to Tanis, located near the Nile River delta. As a result, the royal tombs were adapted to the new surroundings. Little rock existed in which to cut a tomb, so they consisted instead of stone tombs sunk into the ground.

When the country was reunited sometime around 700 BC, rock-cut tombs reappeared, both in the capital of Thebes and in the north at Saqqara. Many of the northern tombs, however, used a very different design. Instead of being narrow, the shafts descending to the burial chamber were wide, deep pits. The sarcophagi were lowered into the pit, which was then filled to the top with sand to deter grave robbers, who would have to remove thousands of cubic feet of sand to reach their goal.

The era of purely Egyptian tombs came to an end in about 300 BC, when the country became part of the empire of Alexander the Great. From this time on, tomb architecture became a mix of traditional Egyptian with Greek, and later, Roman influences. Even the artwork inside the tombs changed. Gods appear in togas or even Roman armor and can be identified only by their crowns.

> **DID YOU KNOW?**
> The Great Pyramids were not built by slaves, as is often thought, but by skilled workers who lived in temporary villages at the site.

TOMB ARTWORK

Artwork was just as important to the tomb as architecture, and it also mirrored the Egyptians' view of the world. Painting and carving on chapels and temples located aboveground, in the land of the living, tended to portray scenes from everyday life. Those in the burial vault related more to the underworld.

Tomb artwork was much more than mere decoration, having religious and magical overtones. In ancient Egypt, to portray something was to make it "real." Scenes might involve activities that a person had particularly enjoyed, ensuring that he or she would continue to do so in the underworld. Such activities as farming, baking, and butchering were frequently pictured, as were food products, thereby assuring the deceased would have plenty to eat.

Thus scenes in a chapel showing events in the person's life meant those things might have happened as pictured, might be idealized scenes of actual events, or might be events that would occur in the afterlife. This was especially true of kings, whose exploits in warfare were frequently exaggerated. This was done not only to glorify the king but also to show that he had worked against the forces of evil in order to bring *ma'at* to the country.

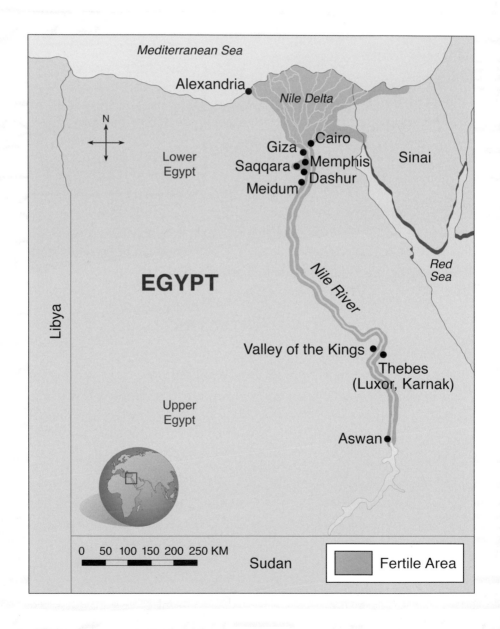

THE CYCLE IN ARTWORK

The same idea carried over to scenes of everyday life in the nonroyal tombs. Agricultural scenes might indicate food for the afterlife, but on a deeper level they were connected with the essential concept of the cycle of the seasons—death and rebirth.

Artwork in burial chambers and nearby passageways, on the other hand, was not intended for viewing by visitors. Instead, it was designed to aid the deceased on their journeys through the Duat. The Coffin and Pyramid texts, for instance, were situated so that when the dead rose from their sarcophagi, they would begin reading at the start and continue around the burial chamber and into the passageway as they ascended. Artwork became more elaborate with the passage of time and came to include full illustrations of the spirit's journey.

There were almost no carvings or paintings concerning the journey through the underworld in nonroyal burial chambers during the early centuries when Egyptians believed that the magical journey was reserved for kings. Rather, the emphasis was on scenes from everyday life. Later, however, the same kinds of illustrations appeared in private tombs, with the exception that commoners were not pictured as joining the company of the gods as were pharaohs.

Although some types of scenes became almost standard, a person had much discretion in how a tomb was to be decorated. He or she might admire the artwork in the tomb of a friend or relative and want something similar. Ikram and Dodson propose that tomb artists might have had catalogs showing scenes they had executed and from which the tomb owner might choose.

The tomb owner had little choice, however, over the most important aspect of burial. Although price dictated some differences, practices were much the same from person to person, except for royalty. This was the first step in the journey to the afterlife, the preservation of the body as a mummy.

Mummification

The ancient Egyptians believed that eternal life in the underworld depended on continuing existence on Earth. Although people might be kept "alive" through statues, an inscription of their names, or simply having their names spoken, the surest way to maintain the *ka, ba,* and all that made up the spirit was to maintain the physical self. To this end, the Egyptians paid just as much attention to preserving their bodies as they did the tombs where they would ultimately rest.

No one knows whether the legend of Osiris's resurrection by Isis gave rise to mummification or whether it was the other way around. Experts suspect that when the Egyptians saw how the desert sand preserved bodies, they began seeking ways to improve the process.

Just when intentional mummification began is still debated. Egyptologists once pointed to the Third Dynasty (about 2663–2597 BC) as a probable starting point. They had to revise their estimate in 1997, however, when excavations in a cemetery about 60 miles (97km) south of ancient Thebes revealed mummies about 1,000 years older.

The exact process of mummification is also open to speculation. Those who practiced and perfected the art left no "how-to" manuals. The Greek historian Herodotus, writing during the fourth century BC, gave the most detailed description. Two other writers, Diodorus of Sicily (about 80 BC) and Porphyry of Tyre (about AD 300), added a few details. All other knowledge has come from a few tomb paintings and by studing the mummies themselves.

BASIC STEPS

The basic steps in mummification involved washing the body, removing some of the internal organs, drying the body, anointing it with sweet-smelling spices, stuffing it for shape, and finally wrapping it for burial. The process underwent many changes over the centuries. Within each step there were variations from century to century and from location to location.

Not every body received every step. As with the tomb, much depended on how much the deceased or their families could afford. Herodotus wrote that there were three general categories of mummification: one for the wealthy, one for more ordinary citizens, and one for the poor. Embalmers showed prospective clients scale models made from wood representing the categories from which the clients could choose.

After a person died, relatives took the body to a complex called the *per ankh*, or "house of life," that contained the facilities for mummification. The first step took place at the *ibw*, where it was washed. These tents or temporary structures were usually located close to both a source of water, such as the Nile, and the cemetery. In addition to water, the body was rubbed with palm wine that was about 14 percent ethyl alcohol—good for killing bacteria.

> **DID YOU KNOW?**
> The mummification descriptions of both Herodotus and Diodorus refer to natron "baths," but modern experiments have shown that natron was used in its solid, not liquid, form.

EMBALMING

The body was then turned over to the embalmers, who worked in more permanent structures known as *wabt wat* ("pure place") or *per nefer* ("beautiful house"). Unlike other cultures, which shunned people who worked with the dead, the ancient Egyptians considered embalmers to be highly skilled craftsmen. They had their own guilds and probably kept the details of their art secret, except when it came time to pass the information on to successors. Diodorus wrote that the people considered them "worthy of every honour and respect, associating with the priests and being admitted to the temples without hindrance as holy men."[7]

The embalmers normally worked while squatting next to low tables. These tables were only about 20 inches (51cm) high and were lower at one end to permit drainage. Most were made from wood. The corpse rested on four rectangular wooden blocks so that drying material could be placed both beneath and atop the body.

The mummification process, by tradition, lasted 70 days, perhaps because the star Sirius, associated with Anubis, god of the underworld, disappeared from view for a 70-day period during the year. Evisceration—the removal of internal organs—lasted about 15 days. Forty days were required to dry the body and an additional 15 to wrap it.

EVISCERATION

The first step, evisceration, was probably introduced sometime around 2600 BC and, as with most aspects of mummification, changed over time. According to Herodotus, the brain was removed first and was then thrown away because the Egyptians had no idea of its function. One method to remove the brain involved the use of a long metal instrument with a hook on the end. Embalmers used the tool to break through the ethmoid bone, located at the bridge of the nose, and then either scraped the brain away from the skull or stirred it until it was liquid enough to be poured out through the nose. What could not be removed was washed out with palm wine mixed with the sweet-smelling resin frankincense. Afterward the cavity was filled with resin derived from the sap of cedar, fir, or pine trees.

The embalmers took greater care with the organs they thought the person would need in the afterlife. According to Diodorus, a low-level

Bronze surgical knives, on display at the Science Museum in London, may have been used to remove organs during the process of mummification. To remove the brain, ancient Egyptian embalmers used a long metal instrument with a hook on the end.

priest known as a scribe marked a spot for incision, usually somewhere on the lower left side of the body. Then another worker, called the cutter or slitter, made the incision using a knife made of obsidian, or volcanic glass. Once the incision was made, Diodorus wrote, the cutter went through a ritual in which he fled and was pursued by his colleagues, who threw stones at him for defiling the body.

The intestines, stomach, lungs, and liver were removed to be dealt with later. The heart, however, was either left in the body cavity and sewn to the skin or was removed, mummified separately, and later returned to the body. The heart was considered to be the source of a person's spirit, and a major part of Egyptian belief had to do with a weighing of the heart by the gods after death.

The ancient Egyptians considered mummification essential if one were to have a chance to enjoy the afterlife. And, as with most essential things, it could be very costly. A surviving tally of what one customer's family was charged runs to nearly 370 drachmas, which was a Greek monetary unit used in Egypt from about 330 BC to AD 40. Comparisons of ancient and modern monetary values are difficult to make, but this was a considerable sum. One could buy a high-quality slave for 300 drachmas and a small house for 400.

One reason for the high cost was that the equipment, once used, became sacred to the memory of the deceased and could not be used again. When the mummy was completed, any leftover material, such as linen, oil, or paint, was buried.

The most expensive item on the list, linen cloth, accounted for 132 drachmas, more than a third of the total. Other high-cost items included the mummy's mask at 34 drachmas, hired mourners at 36 drachmas, an old tunic—the purpose of which is unknown—and cedar oil at 41 drachmas. Least expensive was an earthenware pot at 4 *ob*, an *ob* being one-sixth of a drachma.

THE DIVINE SALT

After evisceration the body was washed once more with water and palm wine before the drying process began. Embalmers packed the body on all sides with a salt known as natron—a mixture of four sodium compounds found naturally near the Nile Delta. They also placed bags of natron in the body cavity to absorb moisture there. The

Egyptians referred to natron as *netjry*, or "divine salt," and it acted on the body by both drying it out and dissolving the fatty tissues.

The natron was changed periodically as it soaked up fluids and fat. When the drying was completed, the body was washed a final time, after which the cavity might be filled with some substance to help it retain its shape. Sawdust, rags, grain chaff, and leaves were among the various stuffing materials used. Workers then sewed up the incision and anointed the body with costly, aromatic oils. Occasionally liquefied resin was poured over the body both to aid in preservation and to hold in place some magical charms placed on the body.

Embalmers went through all these steps only with those who could afford the entire process. According to Herodotus's description of the second option for embalming, no incision was made. Instead, he writes that "oil of cedar [probably turpentine made from juniper] is injected with a syringe into the body through the anus which afterwards is stopped up to prevent the liquid from escaping."[8] The body was then kept in natron for about 40 days, after which the liquid was allowed to drain out, carrying the internal organs with it. There is no mention of wrapping the corpse in cloth.

> **DID YOU KNOW?**
> The 70-day timeline for mummification is referred to in the Bible. According to the book of Genesis, Jacob, the father of Joseph, died in Egypt and was embalmed over a 40-day period while Egyptians mourned for him for 70 days.

TREATMENT OF THE POOR

Apparently the poor were not wrapped either. Instead, they only had their intestines flushed out and then were dried in natron. They were usually buried in a sand pit, sometimes wrapped in the sleeping mat they had used in life.

Wrapping, however, was the next step for the wealthy, and it involved an entirely new set of workers. It was considered a sacred process, filled with rituals, and thus was done by priests. They were led by the *hery sesheta*, or "overseer of mysteries," who wore a mask of the god

Anubis. His role was to direct the others, and he seems not to have done much of the actual work because the mask interfered with his vision. Most of the wrapping was done by priests called the *hetemw netjer*, or "high priest;" meanwhile, another type of priest, the *here heb*, or "reader priest," read the proper prayers and spells aloud as the wrapping progressed.

The priests not only did the wrapping but also included charms and other magical symbols within the wrapping. They might write prayers on the strips of linen and, at the same time, recite those prayers. For instance, instructions in the Book of the Dead tell the priests precisely what is to be recited

> over a figure of Horus, made of lapis-lazuli, which shall be placed on the neck of the deceased. It is a protection upon earth, and it will secure for the deceased the affection of men, gods, and the Spirit-souls which are perfect. Moreover it acted as a spell in Khert-Neter [the underworld], but it must be recited by thee on behalf of the Osiris Ra, regularly and continually millions of times.[9]

THE POWER OF AMULETS

The charms, known as amulets, took many forms and served many purposes. They were intended to protect the mummy from harm, aid the deceased on the journey through the underworld, and to take the place of a body part should one be damaged or lost. They might derive their power from their shape, color, the substance from which they were made, spells carved on them, or spells recited over them.

Scarabs were among the most popular amulets and most often were shaped like the beetle *Scarabaeus sacer*, which to the Egyptians was a symbol of resurrection. The most important scarab was the one placed over the heart as a priest prayed that the heart would receive a favorable judgment in the afterlife.

The *Wadjet* eye, or Eye of Horus, was another popular and powerful amulet. It was intended to provide protection from harm and to ward off curses, not only for the dead in the afterlife but also for the living on Earth. It was worn by Egyptians from the earliest recorded times to well beyond the Roman period and may have been retained in some form by Christians and Muslims as those religions spread into the country.

LAYERS OF AMULETS

Priests placed amulets on the body in two general layers: inner and outer. The amulets on the inner layer were more numerous and were made mostly from stone. The amulets on the outer layer were either a glazed pottery known as faience or glazed, semiprecious stones such as lapis lazuli, jasper, or quartz.

The number of amulets used increased over time. Early mummies might contain 10 or 15, but later ones included about 55. The mummy of the pharaoh Tutankhamun, who died in about 1336 BC, had 143 amulets, possibly because—as modern science has shown—he was extremely frail and sickly.

Ironically, the amulets intended to protect the mummies often were the cause of their destruction. Tomb robbers tore mummies apart and sometimes burned them in order to reach the more valuable charms, especially the heart scarab.

> **DID YOU KNOW?**
> Ahmose II, who died in about 1524 BC, is the first mummy known to have had his brain removed during mummification. It was not removed through the nose, however, but by creating an opening between the spinal cord and skull.

The linen cloth in which amulets were placed began to be used at about the same time that artificial mummification began. For about the first 1,700 years of mummification, wrappings were not fine linen made especially for that purpose, although those intended for royalty could have been. Instead, they were normally strips cut from sheets or old clothes belonging to the deceased, sometimes carrying laundry marks bearing the owner's name.

A SIGN OF HUMILITY

Wrapping someone's body in old clothes was not a form of disrespect; it was intended to demonstrate the transitory nature of life on Earth. In some ceremonies, the final words spoken by relatives before a mummy's tomb was sealed were "the good shepherd has gone to the land of Eternity; he who willingly opened his feet to going is now enclosed, bound and confined. He who had so much fine linen, and so gladly put it on, sleeps now in the cast-off garments of yesterday."[10]

The cloth strips were frequently soaked in a natron solution to produce further drying and might also have been dipped in a mild resin solution or coated with oil to hold them in place. These would also act as a glue to secure the charms placed at various points on the body.

As each part of the body was treated, a priest recited the proper lines of prayer: "For you comes the oil! It brings life to your mouth,

During mummification, each limb was wrapped separately. The positioning of the arms varied. In many instances, the arms were crossed over the chest as can be seen on the mummy of New Kingdom pharaoh Thutmose IV.

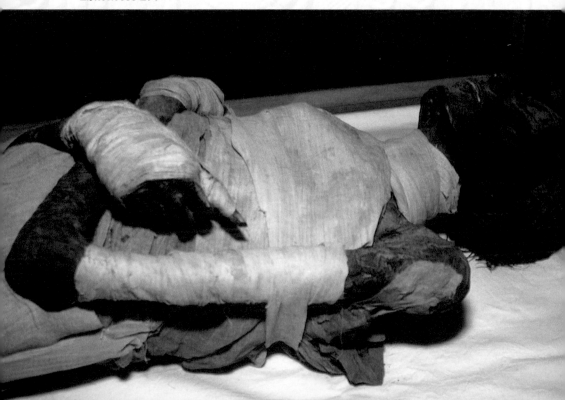

sight to your eye.... It gives you ears to hear what you like.... It gives your nose to inhale the festal perfume.... It gives you your mouth after having provided it with its discernment, like the mouth of Thoth [god of wisdom], which discerns what is just."[11]

Each limb was wrapped separately, with the head and neck coming first. Each finger and toe was individually wrapped, followed by the arms, legs, and—in the case of males—the genitalia. At this point the various charms were put in place and prayers recited. Finally, the legs were tied together with linen pads between them and the arms were positioned.

THE POSITION OF THE ARMS

The arms were placed in various positions throughout the history of mummification. They might be at the sides, crossed over the abdomen, crossed over the pubic area, or crossed over the chest. Sometimes the position was a combination, such as one arm at the side and one over the chest. Palms were usually flat, although some pharaohs had their fists clenched as if still grasping a shepherd's crook and a flail, the Egyptian symbols of kingship.

The torso was the last of the body to be wrapped. For centuries, this was the extent of wrapping. A major change took place sometime around 2200 BC. After all the individual parts were covered, the entire mummy was wrapped again in a spiral from head to feet and then wrapped with a large shroud or shrouds held together with long strips. The shrouds were made from a type of linen different from the usual wrapping cloth and were sometimes colored red for men.

The wrapping process could consume a considerable amount of cloth—4,036 square feet (375 sq. m) of linen for just one mummy. A mummy from the Eighteenth Dynasty, unearthed by archaeologists, was wrapped with 14 sheets, 80 cloth strips, 12 cloth pads, and 4 sets of long cloth strips. Egyptologists spent four days unwrapping this mummy, determined to be the mother of a pharaoh. Some of the wrappings from mummies during a later period, about 500 BC, could weigh up to 60 pounds (27kg).

THE GRECO-ROMAN PERIOD

During this later time, when Egypt was dominated by Greece and Rome, less attention was paid to preservation of the body and more to wrappings. Mummification reached its technical peak in about 1000 BC, after which the quality of embalming declined. Wrappings, however, grew more intricate and elaborate. Shrouds were often multicolored and painted with likenesses of the deceased, figures of gods, or scenes from the Book of the Dead.

The most elaborate wrapping took place during the Roman period (30 BC to AD 395). External cloth strips were laid down in a crisscross pattern, resulting in a series of recessed parallelograms in the middle of which might be a golden stud or button. In some mummies, the cloth strips making up two sides of the parallelogram were colored, with red and pink being the most popular colors.

> **DID YOU KNOW?**
> The mummy of King Ramesses III was the first known to have artificial eyes. The eye sockets were packed with linen to provide a more lifelike appearance.

Mummification was designed to make the final results resemble the deceased as much as possible, especially the facial features. Some early burials left the face unwrapped, and linen soaked in plaster was molded over it and painted. This was replaced by a helmet-like mask that remained in use until the Roman era. Early masks covered only the head. In later periods masks covered much of the chest and upper back as well as the front, and they sometimes extended down the entire length of the body.

THE POWER OF THE MASK

The mask was more than mere decoration. "Masks were intended to help the dead move from the mortal to the immortal world and to protect the physical body from harm," writes art historian Laura Evans. "If the body happened to be destroyed, the soul would be restless for all eternity. In addition, death masks helped to form the soul's face in the afterlife."[12]

ANIMAL MUMMIES

Human beings were by no means the only living creatures mummified in ancient Egypt. The practice was extended to a wide variety of animals. Some were favorite pets buried with their masters so as to provide companionship in the afterlife, but most were mummified for religious reasons specific to a god they represented.

Many gods in ancient Egypt were represented by animals. Horus was a falcon, Hathor a cow, Anubis a jackal or dog, and so on. The various gods were often most sacred to individual towns. Priests serving gods would raise the sacred animals, kill them in a ritual, mummify them, and sell them to worshippers.

One notable exception was the bull Apis, a manifestation of the god Ptah. The Apis was one of the oldest religious symbols in ancient Egypt and, as an emblem of fertility and prosperity, was the most revered. Only one bull at a time, chosen according to very specific criteria, could be the Apis, whereas any cat could represent the goddess Bast.

Each Apis led a life of luxury, with his own residence, priests to wait on him, and a harem of selected cows. When he died, he was mummified and buried, sometimes in a huge gallery with some of his predecessors. As priests roamed the countryside in search of the new Apis, the people mourned, only to rejoice when a successor was identified.

Masks were made of various materials. Early ones consisted of linen soaked in plaster, but later versions were crafted from beaten metal, using gold for royalty and those who could afford it. The earliest metal masks tended to be smooth, but over time they evolved into molded metal masks to look more lifelike. Glass and gemstones might be added to furnish color and decoration.

The mask of Tutankhamun, for example, is one of the most famous and most recognized works of art in human history and has been called "staggeringly beautiful"[13] by experts. It features a supposed likeness of the young pharaoh made of gold surrounded by a headdress of gold, blue faience, colored glass, carnelian, lapis lazuli, and translucent quartz.

> **DID YOU KNOW?**
> Porphyry of Tyre is the only ancient source to refer to the storage of the deceased's internal organs in a canopic chest.

When the mask was in place, the mummy was almost ready for the journey to the tomb. But first, special consideration was given to four of the body's organs that had been removed. Unlike the brain, the intestines, stomach, liver, and lungs were considered vital parts of the body and would undergo a separate form of mummification. They were packed in natron to dry or, in some cases, were placed in a solution of natron and water. Throughout most of ancient Egyptian history, the organs were wrapped with the same kind of linen strips used on the body.

CANOPIC CHESTS AND JARS

The mummified organs were placed in canopic chests or in canopic jars. The earliest known canopic chests date from about 2550 BC and were fixtures in ancient Egypt from then on. They were fashioned from wood for private citizens. Those for royalty were carved out of stone, including calcite, quartzite, and granite. They were almost uniformly placed at the feet of the deceased.

The interiors were divided into four quadrants, one for each organ. In early burials the mummified organs were deposited into their respective quadrants without any other container. In some cases the mummified bundles featured a small mask, probably representing the face of the deceased.

Painted wooden canopic jars representing the sons of the god Horus protected internal organs removed during mummification. From left are the baboon-headed Hapy, protector of the lungs; the jackal-headed Duamutef, protector of the stomach; the falcon-headed Qebehsenuef, protector of the intestines; and the human-headed Imseti, protector of the liver.

The jar lids at first were flat or domed; later they were fashioned into the figures of human heads. The human heads eventually gave way to the hawk-headed Horus and later to images of the four sons of Horus: Imseti, Hapy, Duamutef, and Qebehsenuef. Each of these was associated with a particular organ. Human-headed Imseti protected the liver. Hapy, pictured as an ape, held the lungs. Duamutef, represented by a dog, and Qebehsenuef, a falcon, were in charge of the stomach and intestines, respectively.

In about 1700 BC the exteriors of canopic chests featured on each side a jackal representing different aspects of the god Anubis. Starting in about 1550 BC, however, the jackals began to be replaced by four guardian goddesses: Isis, Nephthys, Neith, and Selqet. They were sometimes pictured facing each corner, their arms extending down the sides in a protective gesture. They also might face outward from each corner and have wings extending down the sides. In the case of Tutankhamun's tomb, the goddesses are statues facing inward on each side of the chest, their arms extended in a protective embrace.

When preservation of both the body and the internal organs had been completed, the mummy was ready for the next steps: the journey to the tomb and—it was hoped—the journey to paradise and immortality.

CHAPTER 3

The Two Journeys

Seventy days after a person's relatives had conveyed his or her body to the house of life, it was returned to them as a mummy, anointed with oils, wrapped in cloth strips, covered with spells, and accompanied by the canopic jars. The deceased would then undertake two journeys. The first was to the tomb, in the company of those who had known the person on Earth. The second was much more perilous—through the underworld to the place where the heart would be weighed and judgment pronounced by the gods.

To the ancient Egyptians, the two journeys were continuations of the one that had begun at birth and, they hoped, would last through eternity. Death was merely a necessary part of the path. "Of all ancient societies, none was more concerned to defeat death than the ancient Egyptians," writes British Egyptologist John H. Taylor. "[Death was] accepted as a transition that had to be passed through to reach eternal life."[14]

The funeral, or day of burial, was an important part of this transition. Although it was a day of mourning, it was also one of celebration with the deceased magically brought back to life, at least in spirit. It was, according to one ancient account,

the passing into reveredness. A night is made for you with ointments and wrappings from the hand of Tait [goddess of weaving]. A funeral process is made for you on the day of burial; the mummy case is of gold, its head of lapis lazuli. The sky is above you as you lie in the sled, oxen drawing you, musicians going before. The dance of the *muu*-dancers is done at the door of your tomb; the offering-list is read to you; sacrifice is made before your offering stone.[15]

Many depictions of funeral processions have survived. One of the most detailed is that of Ani, a scribe who is thought to have died in about 1250 BC. His funeral forms much of the illustration of the Book of the Dead written for him. A priest with a panther skin draped over his shoulders leads the way. A pair of oxen and four men pull a sledge—a vehicle on runners—on which the coffin rests.

The coffin is enclosed in a catafalque, or platform, shaped like a shrine—an indication that the deceased was headed for a union with the gods. Part of the catafalque is shaped like a boat, symbolizing the

Ancient Egyptians take part in a funeral procession. The funeral was both a day of mourning and a day of celebration, with mourners grieving their loss but also celebrating the return to life of the spirit of the deceased.

golden boat on which the sun god Ra was thought to sail across the sky. Two goddesses are there for protection: Isis in the bow and Nephthys in the stern. Ani's widow, Tutu, is shown kneeling beside the catafalque, looking up at the coffin. She is dressed for mourning, wearing a blue-gray garment that leaves the breasts bare. A tear is falling from her eyes.

ESCORTS TO THE TOMB

Eight men, probably relatives and friends, walk close behind the coffin, also wearing expressions of sorrow. At the rear of the procession, servants drag a sledge carrying the canopic chest, on which sits a jackal, the symbol of Anubis. Other servants carry household goods the deceased will need in the afterlife, including a bed and a chair.

One servant carries two small statues. These are the *shabti*, a word thought to mean "followers" or "answerers." The Egyptians believed that activities in the afterlife mirrored those on Earth, including such manual labor as farming or fishing. The *shabti* represented workers who would perform such tasks for

> **DID YOU KNOW?**
> The construction of a pharaoh's tomb began at the time he began his rule. No matter how long he reigned, however, it was never completely finished until after he died. To do so would have been seen as hastening his death.

the deceased. In the Book of the Dead, a spell instructs the *shabti* to "plough the fields, or to fill the channels with water, or to carry sand. . . . The Shabti Figure replieth: I will do it, verily I am here [when] thou callest."[16]

Eight women greet the procession as it nears the tomb. Like Tutu, they are dressed in mourning. They are weeping and their arms are upraised in grief. They are probably professional mourners hired for the occasion, a practice still common in Egypt and many other countries. Though not pictured, *muu* dancers might have met the procession along the way, performing ritual dances to the sound of wooden clappers.

The final scene depicts Ani's coffin being stood upright at the tomb entrance, facing the sun and supported from behind by a priest wearing a mask representing Anubis. Tutu kneels before the mummy as the lead priest performs the most important ritual of the day—the Opening of the Mouth ceremony.

OPENING OF THE MOUTH

Up to this point the mummy had been considered a lifeless, inanimate object. The Opening of the Mouth ceremony was intended to bring it back to life. There might be as many as 100 steps during the ritual, but the key moment came when a *sem* priest, usually the oldest son of the deceased, touched the mummy's mouth, ears, and eyes with special tools. One such tool used as a symbol of rebirth was the *pesesh-kef* knife, the same kind of implement used to sever a baby's umbilical cord at birth. At this moment the *sem* priest would chant:

> [Name]! I have opened your mouth for you. [Name]! I open your mouth for you with the nua-blade. I have opened your mouth for you with the nua-blade, the meskhetyu-blade of iron, that opens the mouths of the gods. . . . Horus has opened the mouth of [Name] with that with which he opened the mouth of his father, with which he opened the mouth of Osiris with the iron that came from Seth, the meskhetyu-blade of iron with which the mouths of the gods are opened.[17]

The ceremony was important not only because it was thought to restore the deceased to life but also because it restored the senses, especially speech, which would be vital in the upcoming journey through the underworld. In one spell the deceased says, "My mouth has been given to me that I may speak with it in the presence of the Great God."[18]

After the ceremony relatives carried the coffin to the burial chamber. Instructions and spells to guide the deceased through the under-

DANCING AT THE FUNERAL

Throughout much of ancient Egyptian history— roughly from 2570 to 1070 BC—groups known as *muu* dancers were a fixture at private funerals. They are pictured frequently in tombs, dressed in a distinctive head-dress of woven papyrus stems from which a cone-shaped structure comes to a point and then flares outward.

In most representations they first meet the funeral at the Hall of the Muu on the edge of the necropolis or cem-etery. They appear next at the point where priests load the sarcophagus onto the barge-shaped sledge, then again at a point in the cemetery called the Gates of Buto. They make their final appearance when the canopic jars containing the deceased's internal organs reach the tomb.

No clear evidence exists to explain what the *muu* danc-ers represented or why they performed at certain points during the funeral. That they danced as the sarcophagus was loaded might mean they represented the ferryman who would take the deceased down a river in the under-world. The significance of dancing at the Gates of Buto could possibly have been to honor former kings because Buto was another name for the cobra god that signified royalty. Likewise, in meeting the canopic jars at the tomb, the dancers might have represented the four sons of Horus said to guard each jar.

world and depictions of the idyllic life found there frequently appeared on the chamber walls. Other spells were intended to protect both the mummy and tomb, including four unbaked mud bricks, each of which had a figure intended to ward off evil.

THE SEALING OF THE TOMB

Once the coffin was lowered into the stone sarcophagus and the lid placed on top, servants brought in the canopic chest along with all the household goods, food offerings, and any implements that might be needed in the afterlife, such as oars or weapons. Afterward the chamber was sealed. A large stone or boulder might be placed over the entrance and the shaft from above filled with sand to deter would-be robbers.

Once above ground, friends and relatives might share a meal honoring the deceased, who—now in the silence of the burial chamber—was about to begin the journey through the underworld.

The elaborate rituals that surrounded death, mummification, and burial underscored the importance the ancient Egyptians placed on the afterlife. "Everything depended on the Egyptian belief in eternal life, and the need to provide for it," write Egyptologists Salima Ikram and Aidan Dodson. "This had nothing to do with a morbid fascination with death. Far from it—it reflected a love of life and a need to ensure that it carried on beyond this world, where life could be all too short."[19]

The universe of the ancient Egyptians consisted of three parts. The first part was the world in which people lived. Second was the sky, personified by the goddess Nut, who arched protectively over the earth and across which Ra sailed each day in his golden boat. Third was the underworld, the Duat, which began in the west where Ra disappeared and extended, below the surface of the earth, to the east where he appeared each morning.

> **DID YOU KNOW?**
> From about 1550 to 950 BC it was common for cuts of meat or entire birds to be mummified and placed in tombs to furnish the deceased with food for the journey through the underworld.

THE FIELD OF REEDS

Part of the underworld—the paradisiacal Field of Reeds—was believed to resemble the populated stretch of fertile land along the Nile

River. There were marshes and fields in which to hunt, fish, or farm. Air and water were just as real there as on Earth. There was sunlight as Ra's boat left the land of the living to illuminate the realm of the dead. Those judged worthy to live there ate, drank, traveled from place to place, hunted, farmed, and even had sex.

But the underworld was also a supernatural place. There were said to be trees made of turquoise in the Field of Reeds, and the sun sometimes sent turquoise rays of light. There was a lake of fire, and mountains and caverns where gods lived. In order to reach the Field of Reeds, the deceased had to journey through a part of the underworld filled with terrors and challenges that could be overcome only with courage and cunning.

The traveler was protected by a host of spells and prayers. One reads, "May I have power in my heart, may I have power in my arms, may I have power in my legs, may I have power in my mouth, may I have power in all my members . . . may I have power over men who would harm me . . . women who would harm me in the realm of the dead."[20]

Other spells were more specific, such as the deceased praying that his heart would not be stolen, that he would not die a second time, that he would not have his head cut off, and that he would not endure many other calamities. One of the greatest fears was that the physical body would decompose inside the tomb. If that happened, according to another spell, "all his bones are corrupt, his flesh is slain, his bones are softened, his flesh is made into foul water, his corruption stinks and he turns into many worms."[21]

PROTECTION FROM ANIMALS

Additional spells furnished protection from wild animals. The deceased must drive away crocodiles who attempt to steal his magic. He or she must use the voice restored by the Opening of the Mouth ceremony. At one point the deceased must repel a snake, telling it to "take yourself off, for Geb [god of the earth] protects me; get up, for you have eaten a mouse, which Ra detests, and you have chewed the bones of a putrid cat."[22]

One of the greatest challenges for the traveler is to pass through seven gates. Each gate is guarded by demons—human figures with heads of animals such as crocodiles, jackals, lions, and rabbits—some of them holding knives. The guardians have names such as He Who Lives on Snakes and Hippopotamus-Faced Raging of Power. Again, it is the power of speech that saves the deceased, who knows the name of each guardian. Speaking the names gives the deceased power over them, and he or she passes through each gate.

The deceased also must pass over 14 mounds inhabited by mysterious animals, including a snake named the Caster of Knives. There are caverns that must be traversed, each with a god who must be appeased with the proper prayer.

> **DID YOU KNOW?**
> Masks were supposed to give mummies the ability to see and a godlike appearance to drive away enemies. Favorite colors were gold and blue, which could consist of gold and lapis lazuli for the wealthy or paint for the poor.

The Book of the Dead and other ancient Egyptian funerary texts do not describe the journey through the Duat in terms of geography or time. There is no map. There is no indication where the gates stand in relation to one another or to the mounds or caverns. There is no prescribed order in which the various challenges are encountered. There are no clues as to how long the journey is expected to take.

THE HOUSE OF OSIRIS

Once the journey is complete, however, and all the obstacles overcome, the deceased reaches the House of Osiris, where still more obstacles await. These are a series of pylons similar to the ones in earthly temples. There are 21 portals, each guarded by mysterious beings with lengthy names such as Lady of Tremblings, Lady of Night Who Tramples the Red Demons, and Hewer-in-Pieces in Blood. Once more, knowing and speaking the names of the guardians allows the deceased finally to reach the place of judgment.

Once the mummification ritual was complete, the body was placed in a coffin which was then lowered into a stone sarcophagus. In the case of Tutankhamun, the body was placed inside an ornate, gold coffin (pictured) which nested in two additional coffins inside the sarcophagus.

The gods' chief criterion in judging a person was whether the person had lived in such a way as to achieve *ma'at*. The place of judgment was known as the Hall of the Two Ma'ats because *ma'at* is pictured as twin goddesses who either guide the deceased or who are sitting near the entrance. It is not clear whether the hall is within the House of Osiris or how it might be reached. The Book of the Dead does say, however, that the deceased should be "cleansed and purified, and is arrayed in linen apparel, and is shod with sandals of white leather, and his eyes are painted with antimony [a silver-white metallic solution], and his body is anointed with unguent made of myrrh [an aromatic resin]."[23]

Before allowing entry, the gods question the deceased. They might want to know the person's name, where he or she had been, what he or she had seen, and much more. Once satisfied, the gods say, "Come, then, and step through this gate of the Two Ma'ats, for you know us."[24]

ADDRESSING THE GATE

Before stepping through the gate, the deceased must speak the names of all its parts, including the door posts, timbers, bolt, hinges, and so forth. Once the gate opens, the deceased steps through and is greeted by Thoth, the god of wisdom. They then have this exchange:

> "Come now," saith Thoth, "for what purpose hast thou come?" [And I reply]: "I have come, and have journeyed hither that my name may be announced [to the god]." [Thoth saith]: "In what condition art thou?" [And I reply], "I, even I, am purified from evil defects, and I am wholly free from the curses of those who live in their days, and I am not one of their number." [Thoth saith]: "Therefore shall [thy name] be announced to the god." [Thoth saith]: "Tell me, who is he whose heaven is of fire, whose walls are living serpents, and whose ground is a stream of water? Who is he?" [And I reply], "He is Osiris."[25]

Everything in the journey thus far has been preliminary. At this point, the gods have found the deceased to have been courageous, knowledgeable, and worthy to enter the Hall of Two Ma'ats. The hall, in most depictions, is a long room, its ceiling supported by columns

A PLACE FOR THOSE WITHOUT SIN

The Field of Reeds was not the only version of an ancient Egyptian paradise. In another version the name for the underworld was Amenti, and it was personified by the goddess of the same name. She was depicted as a woman with the hieroglyphic sign for the west on her head.

Amenti was thought to live at the far western edge of the desert, where she would welcome the dead to their new dwelling place. Although the ancient Egyptians observed a rigorous system of social classes, all people were said to be equal in Amenti, provided they were worthy. One tomb text read: "Amenti is the dwelling place of one without sin: happy is the man who arrives there! No one reaches it save the one whose heart is exact in practicing equity. There, there is no distinction between poor and rich, except in favor of the one who is found to be without sin when the scale and the weight are in front of the Lord of Eternity."

Françoise Dunand and Roger Lichtenberg, *Mummies and Death in Egypt*: Ithaca, NY: Cornell University Press, 2006, p. 71.

much as an earthly chapel or shrine would be. White ostrich feathers, the symbol of *ma'at*, appear frequently among the decorations, as do cobra symbols of royalty.

The major gods—Anubis, Thoth, and Horus—are usually present, and Osiris, king of the Duat, sits or stands at the end of the hall opposite the entrance, sometimes accompanied by Isis, Nephthys, and the four sons of Horus. Later depictions, after 1000 BC, sometimes substitute Ra for Osiris.

THE PROTESTATION OF INNOCENCE

The deceased first proclaims innocence of wrongdoing during his or her earthly life. This Protestation of Innocence is made first to Osiris and then to 42 minor gods, usually pictured as standing in a row. The deceased must know the names of all 42 and the specific action associated with each one. In one part of the lengthy spell, for instance, the deceased says, "Hail Eater of entrails who came forth from the House of Thirty, I have not committed perjury."[26]

> **DID YOU KNOW?**
> Usually about 365 *shabti* statues, one for each day of the year, were placed in a tomb to serve the deceased in the afterlife. Pharaohs could have many more, and one—King Taharqa—had more than 1,000.

The most important part of the judgment—the weighing of the heart—comes next. A large set of scales sits on the floor of the hall. Two pans are suspended from its arms. In one is the heart of the deceased; in the other is a figure of *ma'at*, represented by the white ostrich feather or a squatting goddess with the feather on her head. Thoth, represented as a baboon, conducts the ceremony, sometimes sitting atop the scale's central pole. Horus and Anubis sometimes assist him.

Ancient Egyptians believed that the heart, not the brain, was the primary governing force in a person's life. It was believed to direct all thoughts and actions and, in the Duat, to retain all memories of things done during a person's lifetime. The weighing was to determine whether the person's life had been in keeping with *ma'at*—one of balance and harmony. During this part of the ritual, the heart had to speak to the gods. Its answers were guided by a spell intended to ensure that the heart gave a favorable response, even if it were untruthful. This spell, often found on heart scarabs, read, "O my heart of my mother, my heart of my different ages, do not testify against me, do not take sides against me in the Tribunal, do not let the Scale incline against me before the weigher [Thoth], for you are my force, which is in my body, the modeler who gave life to my limbs."[27]

THE DEVOURER OF SOULS

In most depictions the heart passes the test if it exactly balances *ma'at*. If the heart is heavier, however, the deceased has failed and is thrown to the Devourer of Souls, who sits nearby. In various versions of the Book of the Dead, this monster—which is part crocodile, lion, and hippopotamus—either ate the heart, cut the heart from the deceased and then ate it, or ate the entire person.

Osiris, god of the underworld, passes judgment on the deceased, who stands before him with arms raised. With Osiris's blessing the deceased then passes into eternal paradise.

Punishment did not stop there. The unrighteous deceased might be sent to the Slaughtering Place presided over by Sekhmet, a lion-headed goddess whose demonic servants hack the damned to pieces, burn them with unquenchable fire, and submit them to all sorts of eternal tortures. Many experts consider the Slaughtering Place to have been a forerunner of the Christian concept of Hell.

If, however, the heart is found to be in balance with *ma'at*, Thoth announces the verdict: "I have judged the heart of the deceased, and his soul stands as a witness for him. His deeds are righteous in the great balance, and no sin has been found in him. He did not diminish the offerings in the temples, he did not destroy what had been made, he did not go about with deceitful speech while he was on earth."[28]

The assembled gods then also declare the deceased's worthiness, and Horus presents him or her to Osiris, saying, "That which comes from your mouth has been decreed. The Osiris Ani, true of voice, is declared true. He has no evil; he has not sinned before us."[29] And the deceased, now found pure and frequently pictured as raising his or her arms in jubilation, addresses Osiris directly: "Here I am in your presence, O Lord of the West. There is no wrong-doing in my body, I have not wittingly told lies, there has been no second fault. Grant that I might be like the favoured ones in your suite, O Osiris, greatly favoured by the good god, one loved of the Lord of the Two Lands, [the deceased's name] vindicated before Osiris."[30]

> **DID YOU KNOW?**
> Some coffins dating from about 720 to 520 BC were covered inside and out with verses from the Book of the Dead. The idea was to surround the mummy with protection and also to make the spells available for the deceased to read.

TRUE OF VOICE

The deceased is now proclaimed *maa kheru*, or "true of voice." The gods restore the deceased's heart, which is sometimes pictured on a chain around his or her neck. Likewise, the deceased may hold white feathers to signify his or her vindication.

The deceased can now enter the Field of Reeds or perhaps another ancient Egyptian version of paradise. It is uncertain how the deceased journeys from the Hall of Two Ma'ats to the Field of Reeds, but he or she now lives a life free from worry—in the company of the gods, but not one of them. Some Egyptians might go on to become an *akh* and dwell with the gods in the stars, but to reach the Field of Reeds was enough of a goal for most when they prayed:

> Praise to Ra, Lord of the Sky, the Sovereign who made the gods. Worship him in his goodly shape when he appears in the Day-bark [a golden boat]. . . . May you be gracious to me when I see your beauty, having departed from upon earth. . . . May he grant that I see the sun-disc and behold the moon unceasingly every day; may a place be made for me in the solar bark on the day when the god ferries across, and may I be received into the presence of Osiris in the Land of Vindication.[31]

CHAPTER 4

The Fates of the Mummies

For thousands of years, from ancient historians to modern scientists, Egyptian mummies have been a source of fascination, fear, and fantasy. Originally objects of reverence, they have been plundered for their jewelry, ground up for medicine, used to make paint, and burned as firewood. They have been sources of entertainment, with people buying tickets to watch them be unwrapped. The wrappings have been used to make paper. Hollywood has made them villains in a seemingly endless string of horror films. And they lie by the hundreds in museums as people gaze on them in awe.

Since the late 1800s, however, mummies have also been a subject for scholarly research. As the scientists' tools and technology have advanced, so has the world's knowledge about one of its most ancient civilizations.

Knowledge, however, was not the objective of the mummies' worst enemies: tomb robbers. Indeed, some mummies were plundered even before being placed in a tomb. Egyptologist Herbert Winlock wrote of mummies he unwrapped in 1942. As the cloth strips came off, Winlock was surprised to find evidence—including fingerprints—that some ornaments had been removed from under the wrappings. "There can be little question as to what happened here," he wrote. "The mummies had been rifled before they were even completely wrapped, and that must have taken place in the undertakers' own establishment."[32]

TOMB ROBBERS

Most robberies, however, whether ancient or modern, involved getting inside the tomb. Nothing was able to stop the tomb robbers—not blocks of granite, not shafts filled with sand, not guards (who could be bribed). Not even the cruel death meted out to ancient Egyptian tomb robbers—impalement on a sharpened stake—kept them away.

People outside Egypt grew more aware of mummies as the country was taken over by the Persians, Greeks, and Romans in succession. It was during the Greek period, for instance, that Herodotus wrote his famous account of mummification as an aspect of an ancient culture. But it was much later, around AD 1000, that mummies became noteworthy for something completely different: their supposed medicinal qualities.

The entire concept that mummies had healing powers originated from a mistake that gave mummies their name. Before the twentieth century, people believed that the very dark color of most mummies resulted from being coated in bitumen, a tarry substance derived from petroleum. Because the Arabic word for bitumen was *mum*, the mummy coating came to be called *mummia*, which in English became *mummy*. Bitumen had been used as a medicine or balm by early Muslim physicians, so it was assumed that ground-up mummies would also be beneficial. A Persian doctor, Avicenna, who lived sometime around AD 1000, prescribed it for a wide variety of ailments, ranging from coughs to broken bones.

> ## DID YOU KNOW?
> One artist was so upset to find that his paint, called "mummy brown," contained fragments of actual mummies that he took the tubes of paint into his yard and gave them a decent burial.

Eventually *mummia* became popular in medieval Europe. King Francis I of France was said never to go anywhere without a packet of mixed *mummia* and rhubarb. Shakespeare mentioned it in three of his plays. As late as 1937 it showed up on a list of ingredients in the evil stepmother's poison in the Walt Disney movie *Snow White and the Seven Dwarves*.

THE FRENCH INVASION

Europe began to take notice of the mummies themselves as a result of an invasion of Egypt by Napoléon Bonaparte's French army in 1878. Scholars accompanied the soldiers with orders from Napoléon to make a record of what was found. The resulting book, *Description de l'Égypte*, opened the world of ancient Egypt to the fashionable salons of Paris and London. Mummies became all the rage. Some of the French troops brought them home as souvenirs, including mummified heads as gifts for Napoléon and his wife.

The general public, too, wanted to experience mummies and did so through entertainments called unrollings. In the early 1800s Giovanni Belzoni, a one-time circus strongman turned explorer, unwrapped some mummies at a public display. His former assistant, Thomas Pettigrew, continued the practice starting in 1833, unwrapping mummies while delivering lectures. People of all kinds—princes and politicians in addition to many scientists—flocked to buy tickets. Performances were so popular that on one occasion the Archbishop of Canterbury, head of the Church of England, was denied a seat because the room was too full.

> **DID YOU KNOW?**
> Thomas Pettigrew, a professor who charged admission to see mummies "unrolled," was the first person to notice that mummification techniques varied over different periods of Egyptian history.

It was perhaps the sight of the dry, sometimes rotted corpses under the wrappings that made mummies objects of horror. The first book about a mummy being restored to life appeared in 1827. Other writers picked up the theme, including *Little Women* author Louisa May Alcott, who wrote a short story titled "Lost in a Pyramid," and Bram Stoker, author of *Dracula*, who wrote a book about a mummy's curse.

MUMMY MOVIES

It did not take the movies long to discover that audiences liked being scared by mummies. The first such film, *The Mummy of King Ramses,* appeared in France in 1909, and there would be 48 more over the next 100 years.

Still other uses were found for mummies, including an oil paint named Mummy Brown, which listed "pulverized corpse" as an ingredient. A mill in Maine manufactured mummy paper from old wrappings and sold them to butchers to wrap meat. Mummies were burned as firewood in Egypt, where wood is scarce. Dallas's Neiman Marcus department store offered his-and-her mummy cases in a 1971 Christmas catalog.

Alongside the sensational, however, an increasing body of scholarship was slowly being built. Pettigrew was much more than a showman. As professor of anatomy at London's Charing Cross Hospital, his lectures were of a high quality, and his *History of Egyptian Mummies* in 1834 was the first book on Egyptian archaeology published in English.

Nineteenth-century mummy scholars, however, lacked the tools and technology to do little more than observe. British surgeon Augustus Granville performed one of the earliest dissections of a mummy in 1825, finding a large ovarian tumor. Similarly, American physician Samuel George Morton studied and measured mummy skulls in 1844 in an effort to determine the ethnic origins of the ancient Egyptians.

MICROSCOPIC EXAMINATIONS

In 1852 Austrian physician Johann Czermak undertook what was likely the first microscopic examination of mummy tissues, discovering that the deceased had suffered from atherosclerosis, a hardening of the arteries. Since then, scientists have learned that heart disease was more common in ancient Egypt than had been suspected.

During a study between 2005 and 2010, a team in Orange County, California, found the oldest known case of heart disease in the mummy of a woman who died around 1550 BC. "To me it's shocking that people who have entirely different lifestyles would have the same disease we have," comments Greg Thomas, a cardiologist and a member of the research team. "So we're missing something about the cause of atherosclerosis."[33]

The modern era of mummy science began with the discovery of X-rays by German physicist Wilhelm Röntgen in 1895. Only four months later another German physicist, Walter Koenig, published X-ray images of a mummified cat and the knees of a young Egyptian boy's mummy. In 1896 another researcher used X-rays to detect differences between genuine mummies and fakes that were sold to tourists by unscrupulous merchants.

That same year Koenig performed the first full-body X-ray of an Egyptian mummy. Flinders Petrie, the most eminent Egyptologist of the time, did likewise in 1897. The Englishman was delighted with the result, particularly because the process appeared to leave the mummy unharmed. He and other scientists now had a nondestructive method for examining the interior of mummies.

THE X-RAY OF A PHARAOH

The process was considered safe enough to convince Grafton Elliot Smith, a British anatomy professor, that it was time to X-ray a royal mummy. He chose Thutmose IV as his subject, but the Cairo Museum had no X-ray machine. Accordingly, Smith bundled the mummy into a horse-drawn cab for a trip to a nursing home that had the only machine in the city.

The X-ray results were surprising. Egyptologists had believed, based on historical records, that Thutmose IV was about 50 years old when he died. The X-rays, however, were able to reveal the maturity of the king's skeletal structure, indicating that he was much younger—perhaps about 25.

X-ray examinations of mummies increased during the 1920s and 1930s, but these exams were mostly confined to the arms and legs because of equipment limitations. The machines of the time simply lacked the power for the X-rays to penetrate skulls and torsos that were filled with resin. As technology improved, however, scientists began to fill in the picture of health and medicine in ancient Egypt.

They found, for instance, that a large percentage of the population suffered from arthritis, a disease in which the cartilage between joints

The modern era of mummy science began with X-ray images of a mummified cat, similar to the one shown here (which is part of a collection from Paris's Louvre museum). X-rays provided a nondestructive method for the study of mummies.

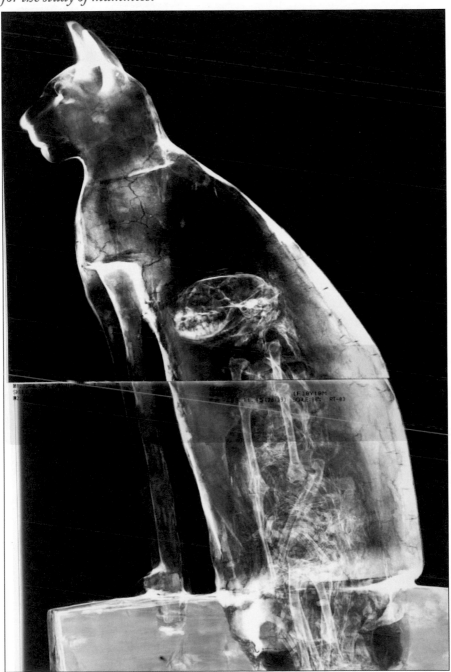

wears away and the bones grind against one another. It affected all classes, and even pharaohs suffered from it. Of the 350 adult mummies found in a large tomb at Saqqara, nearly every one over the age of 30 showed signs of arthritis.

THE TALE OF THE TEETH

Scientists were able to learn much about the age of the individuals at the time of death and about their diet from the condition of their teeth. The degree to which teeth were worn down proved to be a good indicator of age, and X-rays also were able to reveal cavities within the teeth and abscesses penetrating the jawbone. Such painful conditions were much more common among royalty and the wealthy, probably because only they could afford the honey used at the time as a sweetener.

A CT scan of a 2,000- to 2,500-year-old Egyptian mummy, still inside its wrapping, made possible this 3-D rendering of the mummy's skull. Researchers hope CT scans will allow them to determine the age, gender, health, diet, and cause of death of ancient Egyptian mummies.

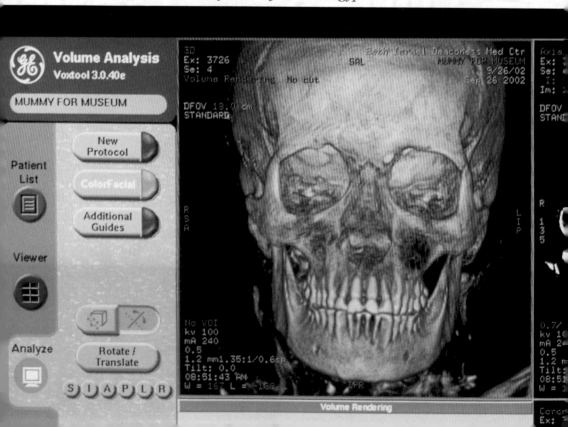

The most common dental problem, however, was that the crowns were worn down over time by the amount of sand and flecks of millstones that worked their way into everyone's food.

The X-rays also showed some evidence of dental work. Fillings made of a combination of resin and chrysocolla, a greenish mineral containing copper, have been found. One Late Period mummy had holes drilled in three teeth that were connected with a gold wire passed through the holes.

While X-ray technology continued to improve, other methods of investigating mummies were being developed as well. Soft tissues—skin, muscles, and internal organs—had been difficult to study because they were no longer soft but dry and brittle after thousands of years in arid tombs. In 1910, however, British pathologist Marc Armand Ruffer, whose specialty was the study of bacteria, developed a method of rehydrating, or moistening, mummified tissue using what came to be called "Ruffer's solution." It consisted of 95 percent alcohol and 5 percent bicarbonate of soda.

> **DID YOU KNOW?**
> The malarial DNA found in Tutankhamun's body is the oldest genetic evidence of the disease ever found.

Using his new technique on kidneys, Ruffer was able to discover eggs of the *Schistosoma haematobium*, a parasite that can cause schistosomiasis, a condition that can lead to bladder cancer and kidney failure, among others. Subsequent studies showed that the condition was common in fishermen, farmers, and others who would have come in contact with stagnant water in which the parasite's larvae swam.

BLOOD TYPING

Another breakthrough occurred in 1933, when American chemist William Boyd found a way to determine the blood types of mummies from small samples of muscle tissue. Three years later American anthropologist P.B. Candela was able to use pulverized bone tissue for similar studies.

There was much to be learned from studying such tissue samples under the microscope, particularly after the development of the electron

THE MUMMY AND THE LAW

Many museums vie with one another to add to their mummy collections. The Brooklyn Museum, however, could not find a way to get rid of one.

When it made the purchase in 1952, the museum officials had wanted the elaborate cartonnage—a painted outer shell, or coffin, made from linen and glue—not the mummy itself. So, when they were able to separate the two, they decided to bury the mummy in the museum garden.

Unfortunately, a policeman saw them and investigated what he thought had been a murder. That misunderstanding was straightened out, but another one took its place. In New York City you cannot bury a body without a death certificate, and this was clearly unobtainable for a mummy that was thousands of years old.

The museum then tried to ship the mummy to another state where a burial might be permitted. Not so fast, said the State of New York. There can be no shipments of bodies out of state without a death certificate.

The museum officials gave up and the mummy, nicknamed "Melvin" by the staff, became a permanent resident. He narrowly escaped being consigned to the museum's incinerator and was put in storage. He emerged in 2010, rewrapped and restored, and on public display for the first time.

microscope. This instrument, instead of depending on direct viewing of an object, uses beams of electrons, which have a far shorter wavelength than do rays of light. Optical microscopes are limited to a magnification of about 200,000, but electron microscopes are capable of producing images that are 2 million times larger than actual size.

Armed with such technology, scientists have identified diseases and other health problems that plagued the ancient Egyptians, such as trichinosis, which is commonly caused by eating meat—chiefly pork—containing the parasite *Trichinella spiralis*. The high number of cases found reveal that pork played a large part in the Egyptian diet.

Other diseases found in ancient mummies include tuberculosis, which was probably acquired through contact with cattle; poliomyelitis; malaria; pneumonia; and smallpox. Smallpox victims include at least one pharaoh, Ramesses V.

ENDOSCOPY

In the early years of mummy research, scientists had to dissect the bodies or at least cut into them to acquire tissue samples. Endoscopy provided a less invasive method. The endoscope is a small light on the end of a long, flexible tube that can be inserted through orifices in the body such as the nose, mouth, or anus. Its early use was limited, however, because a light bright enough to provide good views might generate enough heat to burn the tissues. The invention in the 1960s of the fiber optic endoscope, in which bright but cool light was channeled along glass fibers, made it possible for scientists to examine the tissues closely and snip off small samples.

X-ray technology, however, had not progressed as rapidly. Machines were more powerful, generally able to penetrate skulls and torsos, but it was difficult to see the bones and other objects in relation to one another. What was needed was a three-dimensional X-ray, and that need was filled by computed tomography, now known as a CT scan.

> **DID YOU KNOW?**
> In 1974 the mummy of King Ramesses II was flown to Paris for an examination, after which it was returned to Cairo. It remains the only mummy of a pharaoh known to have left Egypt.

Whereas X-rays are normally taken from two perspectives—one from the side and the other from the back or front—the CT scanner uses a large doughnut-shaped device that takes images from all angles surrounding the body or the portion to be scanned. As the body goes through the machine on a movable table, these images are taken at intervals, with images from each interval constituting a "slice." Computers manipulate the images and slices to produce a three-dimensional image.

THE FIRST MUMMY CT SCAN

Peter Lewin and Derek Harwood-Nash of the University of Western Ontario in Canada performed the first such scan on a mummy in 1977, producing images of the head of Nakht, a weaver who had died in about 1180 BC. A year later Lewin performed the first full-body scan on a female mummy named Djedmaatesankh at Canada's Royal Ontario Museum, but the technology was still in its infancy. "We did it just to show it was possible,"[34] Lewin said.

That technology was much improved when Djedmaatesankh was brought back for a second scan in 1995. Using more modern equipment, the team was able to produce many more images—more, in fact, than would normally be produced from a live patient. "With regular patients, especially with kids, you'd have to worry about radiation dosage,"[35] explains Stephanie Holowka, a technician on the team.

The most interesting part of both scans, from the museum's point of view, was that Djedmaatesankh did not have to be unwrapped or even taken from her cartonnage—a shell-like structure made of linen and glue. "For a museum wanting to show Egyptian art, the decorations are the most important thing," says Royal Ontario Museum curator N.B. Millet. "And the cartonnage is, after all, just a shell. If we had gotten the lady out, we probably would have busted it up pretty badly. It just wasn't worth it."[36]

NEW VIEWS OF ANCIENT DISEASES

CT scans give scientists the ability to make much more detailed observations than have been possible—even down to the cellular level—and those observations have changed the way disease in ancient Egypt is viewed. Cancer previously was thought to be rare in Egyptian mummies. Yet, when a team in Lisbon, Portugal, scanned a mummy dating from about 250 BC, it discovered the oldest known case of prostate cancer in Egypt and the second oldest in the world. The scientists were using a state-of-the-art scanner capable of producing clear images of objects less than a third of a millimeter wide. "I think earlier researchers probably missed a lot without this technology,"[37] asserts radiologist Carlos Prates.

Italian anthropologist Albert Zink agrees. Cancer-causing agents, he says, are not confined to the modern environment, citing such things as soot from wood-burning fireplaces. "I think cancer was quite prevalent in the past," he explains, "more prevalent than we have been able to see."[38]

Portable CT scanners have enabled much more to be seen. Before such instruments were perfected, mummies had to be taken from their location—usually a museum—to a hospital where one of the bulky machines was available. The ability to take the scanner to the mummy rather than the other way around, thus decreasing the possibility of damage to the mummy, has made many more examinations possible.

> **DID YOU KNOW?**
> In 1994 the University of Manchester in Great Britain created the International Ancient Egyptian Mummy Tissue Bank, collecting small samples from various parts of the bodies of a wide range of mummies for use by future researchers.

THE SCAN OF KING TUT

Probably the most famous use of the portable scanner occurred in 2005, when scientists transported one into the Valley of the Kings in the desert west of Luxor. They were there to scan Tutankhamun— "King Tut"—whose discovery in 1924 created a worldwide mummy craze. The mummy, however, had been badly damaged at the time, and a trip to Cairo, 300 miles (483km) to the north, was ruled out.

The scan revealed that what had been indicated by an earlier X-ray—that the pharaoh had been killed by a blow to the back of the head—was incorrect. The skull fracture shown by the earlier

THE QUESTION OF ETHICS

In recent decades officials at museums that put mummies on public display have begun to wrestle with ethical questions. Is what they are doing disrespectful to the ethnic group from which the person comes? Is it disrespectful to the person being studied?

In 1999 anthropologist Karin Wiltschke-Schrotta received a fellowship from the Smithsonian Institution to study the issue. She interviewed museum curators, asking questions such as: Are human remains displayed to educate or to draw visitors? How can human remains be displayed in a dignified manner?

In her final report, Wiltschke-Schrotta cited several things that should be taken into consideration: Are the remains being shown in an appropriate setting, such as a medical museum or science museum where such exhibits might be expected? Are the remains displayed in a respectful manner? Are visitors made aware that human remains are on display?

She contends that the study of mummies and other human beings is an important and valid area of research and that the public deserves an opportunity to view the results of such studies. "As scientists, we must foster the natural human curiosity to learn more about human beings," she concluded.

Karin Wiltschke-Schrotta, "Human Remains on Display: Curatorial and Cultural Concerns," Smithsonian Institution. http://museumstudies.si.edu.

procedure had instead occurred when the body was unwrapped during the 1920s. Nonetheless, Stanford University Egyptologist Kathlyn Cooney asserts that the computerized scans did not necessarily rule out murder. "All this has proved was that there was no blow to the back of the head," she says, adding that "the cause of death is by no means clear."[39]

But more clues about what might have killed Tutankhamun were not long in coming, thanks to a new method of studying mummies: the examination of DNA. This material, contained in cells throughout the body, carries the genes that determine how a living organism will develop and function. Each individual's DNA is different, except for identical twins, and, because genetic material is passed from parents to children, DNA comparisons can establish family relationships.

THE DISCOVERY OF MALARIA

This, indeed, was the objective when Tutankhamun's DNA was studied in 2010 in order to establish his parentage. Scientists, however, were surprised to find not only human DNA but also that of the parasite that causes malaria. In fact, several strains of the parasite's DNA showed up, indicating that Tutankhamun had suffered from malaria multiple times, which might have contributed to his death from a broken leg that had been discovered in the 2005 CT scan.

Egyptian Egyptologist Zahi Hawass, who led both teams, was elated by the discovery: "The results of our DNA analysis . . . convinced me that genetics can provide a powerful new tool for enhancing our understanding of Egyptian history, especially when combined with radiological studies of the mummies and insights gleaned from the archaeological record."[40]

Mummy DNA testing, however, remains controversial. Some scientists contend that mummies are too free of moisture for enough DNA to be collected for a valid study. Others claim there is too much of a risk that mummies could have been contaminated by the DNA of others, either during mummification or after they were discovered.

Although the future of testing ancient DNA may be unclear, it seems likely that science will develop new and as yet undreamed of technologies to unearth secrets and knowledge buried for centuries under the sands of Egypt. Before mummies were entombed, their mouths were ritually opened so that they could speak to the gods. Thanks to science, they still speak to us today.

SOURCE NOTES

CHAPTER ONE: THE EVOLUTION OF RITUAL

1. Quoted in Salima Ikram and Aidan Dodson, *The Mummy in Ancient Egypt*. New York: Thames and Hudson, 1998, p. 15.
2. Quoted in An Introduction to the History and Culture of Pharaonic Egypt, "Body and Soul." www.reshafim.org.il/ad/egypt.
3. Quoted in An Introduction to the History and Culture of Pharaonic Egypt, "Body and Soul."
4. Quoted in An Introduction to the History and Culture of Pharaonic Egypt, "Body and Soul."
5. Quoted in Aidan Dodson and Salima Ikram, *The Tomb in Ancient Egypt*. New York: Thames and Hudson, 2008, p. 13.
6. Salima Ikram and Aidan Dodson, *The Mummy in Ancient Egypt: Equipping the Dead for Eternity*. New York: Thames and Hudson, 1998, p. 22.

CHAPTER TWO: MUMMIFICATION

7. Quoted in James M. Deem's Mummy Tombs, "Diodorus and Mummification in Egypt." www.mummytombs.com.
8. Quoted in Ikram and Dodson, *The Mummy in Ancient Egypt*, p. 104.
9. Quoted in Nazarene Way of Essenic Studies, "Papyrus of Ani; Egyptian Book of the Dead [Budge]." www.thenazareneway.com.
10. Quoted in Ikram and Dodson, *The Mummy in Ancient Egypt,* p. 153.
11. Quoted in Dodson and Ikram, *The Tomb in Ancient Egypt,* p. 98.
12. Laura Evans, "History of Egyptian Masks," Life 123. www.life123 .com.
13. Ikram and Dodson, *The Mummy in Ancient Egypt,* p. 166.

14. John H. Taylor, ed., *Journey Through the Afterlife: Ancient Egyptian Book of the Dead.* Cambridge, MA: Harvard University Press, 2010, p. 12.

15. Quoted in Miram Lichtheim, *Ancient Egyptian Literature: A Book of Readings.* Berkeley and Los Angeles: University of California Press, 1975, p. 229.

16. Quoted in Nazarene Way of Essenic Studies, "Papyrus of Ani; Egyptian Book of the Dead [Budge]."

17. Quoted in University College London, "Contents of the Ritual for 'Opening the Mouth,'" Digital Egypt for Universities. www. digitalegypt.ucl.ac.uk.

18. Quoted in Neil Parker, "The Papyrus of Ani, Chapter 22," Bardo of Death Studies, 1997. www.bardo.org.

19. Ikram and Dodson, *The Mummy in Ancient Egypt,* p. 13.

20. Quoted in Taylor, ed., *Journey Through the Afterlife,* p. 160.

21. Quoted in Taylor, ed., *Journey Through the Afterlife,* p. 160.

22. Quoted in Sarah Bakewell, "Dying like an Egyptian," *Guardian,* November 13, 2010. www.guardian.co.uk.

23. Quoted in Gold Scales, "The Papyrus of Ani: The Egyptian Book of the Dead." http://oaks.nvg.org/eg6ra7.html.

24. Quoted in Taylor, ed., *Journey Through the Afterlife,* p. 206.

25. Quoted in Nazarene Way of Essenic Studies, "The Papyrus of Ani; Egyptian Book of the Dead [Budge]."

26. Quoted in Tour Egypt, "The Declaration of Innocence." www. touregypt.net.

27. Quoted in Françoise Dunand and Roger Lichtenberg, *Mummies and Death in Egypt.* Ithaca, NY: Cornell University Press, 2006, p. 212.

28. Quoted in Taylor, ed., *Journey Through the Afterlife,* p. 212.

29. Quoted in Parker, "The Papyrus of Ani, Chapter 22."

30. Quoted in Carol Andrews, ed., *The Ancient Egyptian Book of the Dead.* Austin: University of Texas Press, 1990, p. 28.

31. Quoted in American Buddha Online Library, "The Egyptian Book of the Dead." http://american-buddha.com.

CHAPTER FOUR: THE FATES OF THE MUMMIES

32. Quoted in Ikram and Dodson, *The Mummy in Ancient Egypt,* p. 61.
33. Quoted in *Orange County Register,* "3,500-Year-Old Mummy Had Heart Disease," April 3, 2011. http:// healthyliving.ocregister.com.
34. Quoted in Kathy A. Svitil, "The Mummy Unwrapped," *Discover Magazine*, April 1, 1995. http://discovermagazine.com.
35. Quoted in Svitil, "The Mummy Unwrapped."
36. Quoted in Svitil, "The Mummy Unwrapped."
37. Quoted in Heather Pringle, "Mummy Has Oldest Case of Prostate Cancer in Ancient Egypt," *Science Now*, October 26, 2011. http://news.sciencemag.org.
38. Quoted in Pringle, "Mummy Has Oldest Case of Prostate Cancer in Ancient Egypt."
39. Quoted in Christopher Joyce, "Head Blow Did Not Kill King Tut, CT Scan Suggests," National Public Radio. www.npr.org.
40. Zahi Hawass, "King Tut's Family Secrets," *National Geographic Magazine*. http://ngm.nationalgeographic.com.

FOR FURTHER RESEARCH

Books

Margaret Bunson, *Encyclopedia of Ancient Egypt*. New York: Facts On File, 2012.

Wendy Christensen, *Empire of Ancient Egypt*. New York: Chelsea House, 2009.

Fergus Fleming, *Ancient Egypt's Myths and Beliefs*. New York: Rosen, 2012.

Kathleen Kuiper, *Ancient Egypt: From Prehistory to the Islamic Conquest*. New York: Britannica Educational, 2010.

Green Roger Lancelyn, *Tales of Ancient Egypt*. New York: Penguin, 2011.

Joyce Tyldesley, *Tutankhamun: The Search for an Egyptian King*. New York: Basic Books, 2012.

Websites

Ancient Egypt (www.ancientegypt.co.uk). This British Museum site is devoted to different aspects of ancient Egyptian culture. Major divisions include mummification, pyramids, gods and goddesses, and temples. One page challenges visitors to make their way through a virtual Egyptian underworld.

Egyptian Mummification (www.spurlock.uiuc.edu/explorations/on line/mummification/index.html). This page, which is hosted by the Spurlock Museum at the University of Illinois at Urbana-Champaign, has sections on mummification history, rituals, and materials.

Egypt's Golden Empire (www.pbs.org/empires/egypt/index.html). This website, created to accompany the Public Broadcasting System's series by the same name, contains a large section on the New Kingdom (sixteenth to eleventh centuries BC). Included are sections on society, religion, and the leading men and women of the time.

Osirisnet (www.osirisnet.net). This nonprofit site is dedicated to describing the tombs and mastabas of ancient Egypt as well as giving information on who was buried within them. Several of the tombs feature three-dimensional virtual tours.

Tour Egypt (www.touregypt.net). Jointly developed in 1994 by the Egyptian Ministry of Tourism and the Egyptian Tourist Authority, this site contains a wide selection of pages devoted to ancient Egyptian history, lifestyles, art, and religion.

INDEX

Note: Boldface page numbers indicate illustrations.

PICTURE CREDITS

Jim Bourg/Reuters/Landov: 62

Richard Chung/Reuters/Landov: 61

© National Geographic Society/Corbis: 42

Frederic Neema/Sygma/Corbis: 11, 34

© Alfredo Dagli Orti/Corbis: 53

© Giani Dagli Orti: 7, 49

SSPL/Science Museum/Art Resource, NY: 29

Thinkstock/Brand X Pictures: 5 (top)

Thinkstock/iStockimages.com: 4

Thinkstock/iStockphotos.com: 5 (bottom left)

Thinkstock/Photos.com: 5 (bottom right)

© The Trustees of the British Museum/Art Resource, NY: 39

© Ron Watts/Corbis: 17

© Roger Wood/Corbis: 21

Steve Zmina: 24

ABOUT THE AUTHOR

William W. Lace is a native of Fort Worth, Texas. He retired in 2011 after 30 years as an administrator at Tarrant County College in Fort Worth and now teaches journalism there. He holds a bachelor's degree from Texas Christian University, a master's degree from East Texas State University, and a doctorate from the University of North Texas. Prior to joining Tarrant County College, he was director of the News Service at the University of Texas at Arlington and a sportswriter and columnist for the *Fort Worth Star-Telegram*. He has written more than 50 nonfiction books for young readers on subjects ranging from the atomic bomb to the Dallas Cowboys. He and his wife, Laura, a retired school librarian, live in Arlington, Texas, and have two children and four grandchildren.